CRASH COURSE IN
CHORDS

BY LEE EVANS

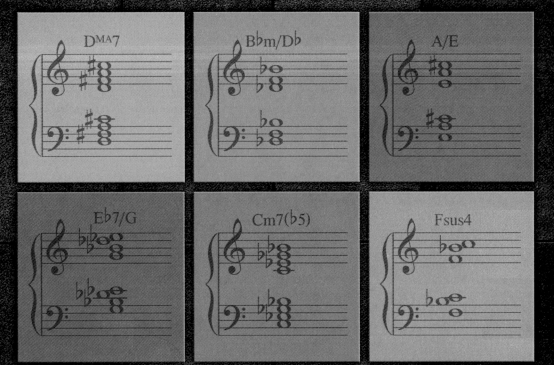

ISBN 978-1-4584-0831-0

HAL•LEONARD®
CORPORATION
7777 W. BLUEMOUND RD. P.O. BOX 13819 MILWAUKEE, WI 53213

In Australia Contact:
Hal Leonard Australia Pty. Ltd.
4 Lentara Court
Cheltenham, Victoria, 3192 Australia
Email: ausadmin@halleonard.com.au

Visit Hal Leonard Online at
www.halleonard.com

PREFACE

The principal goal of *Crash Course in Chords* is to introduce students to the basic theory of chords, chord qualities, and chord functions, with an eye towards laying the groundwork for later practical experiences in chord playing and chord improvisation.

It is necessary for students first to be familiar with major and minor scales and with the nomenclature of intervals in order to speak the language of chords and chord qualities. If students need a review of basic intervals and scales, it is recommended that they begin with the Theory Review on pages 40–48 before beginning this book. If instructors deem it necessary or worthwhile, students may be started on these pages prior to working with the heart of the book that begins on page 4.

This book presupposes early-intermediate level student keyboard skills.

Upon completion of this volume, the student will be amply prepared to proceed to a follow-up book entitled *How to Play Chord Symbols in Jazz and Popular Music*, by Lee Evans and Martha Baker (Hal Leonard Corporation, publisher).

CONTENTS

AN INTRODUCTION TO CHORDS

Chords

The three principal areas of music are melody, rhythm, and harmony. Harmony is created when two or more tones are sounded simultaneously. A chord is any group of three or more tones sounded simultaneously.

Triads

The basic chord of tonal music (music in a particular key and based upon major and minor scales) is the *triad*. The triad is a special type of three-note chord built in intervals of thirds and arranged on the staff in the order of line, line, line, or space, space, space. By virtue of that consecutive line or consecutive space arrangement of three tones on the musical staff, a triad possesses a *root* (the bottom note when the triad is in its basic, or root, position), plus the intervals of a *3rd* and a *5th*. In fact, the bottom note of each such triad is referred to as the root, the tone above it is called the 3rd, and the uppermost tone is called the 5th.

Each triad derives its name from the root tone, and derives its *quality* (major, minor, diminished, augmented) from the intervals between the root and 3rd, and the root and 5th.

The Relationship of Triads to Scales

A *major triad* is derived from the first, third, and fifth notes of a *major scale*. Thus, the C major triad consists of the notes C (root), E (3rd), and G (5th). A major triad consists of a major 3rd (M3) and a perfect 5th (P5). (Another way of looking at a major triad is that it consists of a major 3rd and a minor 3rd.)

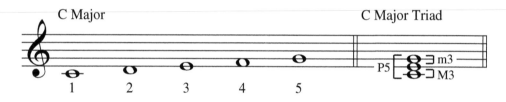

A *minor triad* is derived from the first, third, and fifth notes of a *minor scale*. Thus, the C minor triad consists of the notes C (root), E♭ (3rd), and G (5th). A minor triad consists of a minor 3rd (m3) and a perfect 5th (P5). (Another way of looking at a minor triad is that it consists of a minor 3rd and a major 3rd.)

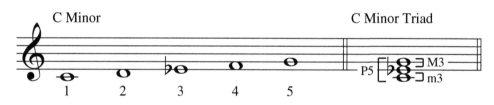

Both the major and minor triads have a perfect 5th (P5). The interval of the 3rd is the only difference between a major and minor triad.

NOTE: In a *major triad*, the 3rd is a *major 3rd* (M3) or *four half-steps*.
In a *minor triad*, the 3rd is a *minor 3rd* (m3) or *three half-steps*.

Writing Major and Minor Triads

Write the following triads in root position on consecutive lines or spaces from the given root note. After you have written all the triads below, play them. That will enable you to hear the vast difference between the sound of major and minor triads.

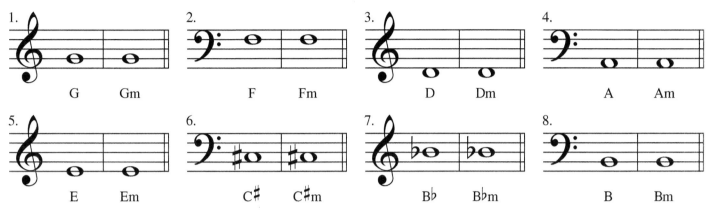

1.	2.	3.	4.
G Gm	F Fm	D Dm	A Am

5.	6.	7.	8.
E Em	C# C#m	B♭ B♭m	B Bm

Diminished Triad

A *diminished triad* consists of a minor 3rd (m3) and a diminished 5th (d5). (Another way of looking at a diminished triad is that it consists of two minor 3rds.)

Augmented Triad

An *augmented triad* consists of a major 3rd (M3) and an augmented 5th (A5). (Another way of looking at an augmented triad is that it consists of two major 3rds.)

Writing Diminished and Augmented Triads

Write the following triads in root position on consecutive lines and spaces from the given root note. After you have written all the triads, play them. This will enable you to hear the vast difference between the sound of diminished and augmented triads.

NOTE: A double sharp (𝄪) or double flat (♭♭) may be required in one or more of these examples.)

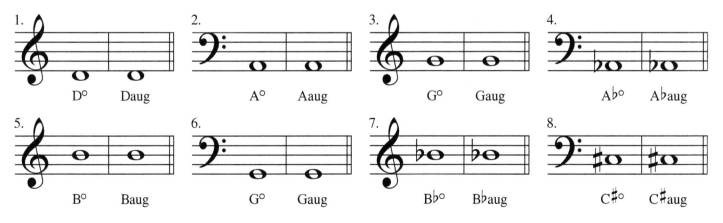

1.	2.	3.	4.
D° Daug	A° Aaug	G° Gaug	A♭° A♭aug

5.	6.	7.	8.
B° Baug	G° Gaug	B♭° B♭aug	C#° C#aug

WRITING TRIADS IN
ALL FOUR CHORD QUALITIES

Write the triads asked for on page 7. In order to make certain that you are building the *major triads* correctly, remember that you will be deriving the notes of the major triad from the first, third, and fifth notes of the major scale. (Refer to the major scales that appear on page 41.)

In order to construct a C *major triad,* extract from the C major scale the first (C), third (E), and fifth (G) notes.

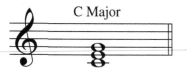

To make a *minor triad* from the major triad, lower the 3rd of the major triad one half-step.

To make a *diminished triad* from a minor triad, lower the 5th of the minor triad one half-step.

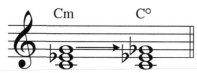

To make an *augmented triad* from a major triad, raise the 5th of the major triad one half-step.

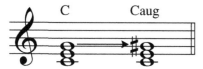

Notation Hints

In the exercises on page 7, do not use enharmonic note names. All triads should remain in their consecutive-line or consecutive-space order. (Occasionally a double sharp (✗) or double flat (♭♭) may be required.)

Also, when notes on two or more consecutive lines or spaces use accidentals, place the accidental adjacent to the highest note close to it. The accidental to the note underneath it should be placed slightly to the left, thus avoiding a crash of accidentals into one another. A third note's accidental is again placed close to the note. Thus, the basic plan of placement of accidentals is: close, away, close, etc.

WRITING TRIADS

Write the triads on this page. The first four are done for you.

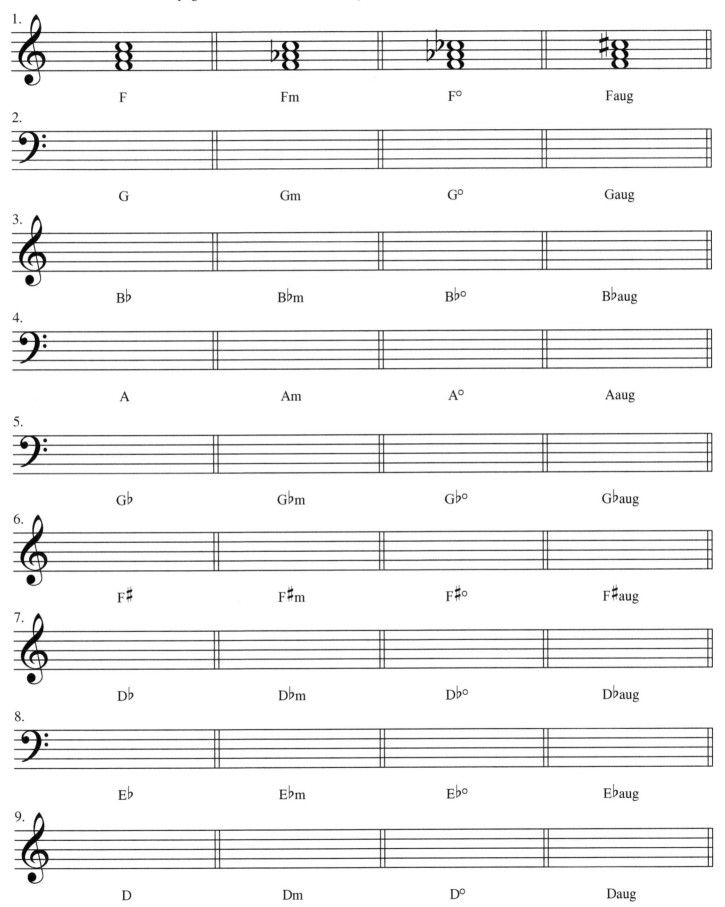

INVERSIONS OF TRIADS

All chords, including triads, may also appear in *inversions*, a rearrangement of the tones of a root-position chord. Below is an A major triad in *root position* followed by the same three notes rearranged into *first inversion*, and then into *second inversion*. Notice that in order to achieve first inversion, one raises the root of the root-position triad one octave, and leaves the other two tones where they are. Similarly, in order to achieve second inversion, one raises the bottom note of the first-inversion triad one octave, and leaves the other two notes where they are.

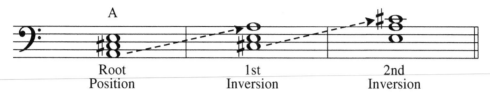

Root Position   1st Inversion   2nd Inversion

Notice that when a triad is in *root position*, the bottom note of the triad is the first note of the scale (A of the A major scale). When a triad is in *first inversion*, the bottom note of the triad is the third note of the scale (C♯ of the A major scale). When a triad is in *second inversion*, the bottom note of the triad is the fifth note of the scale (E of the A major scale).

Triad Inversion Exercises

Name each root-position triad in the box provided. Write the first and second inversions of each of the root-position triads. (**Hint:** Make certain that if a triad in root position employs accidentals, you apply the accidentals to the exact same note(s) in the inversions.) After completing the following written exercises, play the root position and two inversions of each triad consecutively, either separate hands or hands together. The first exercise has been done for you.

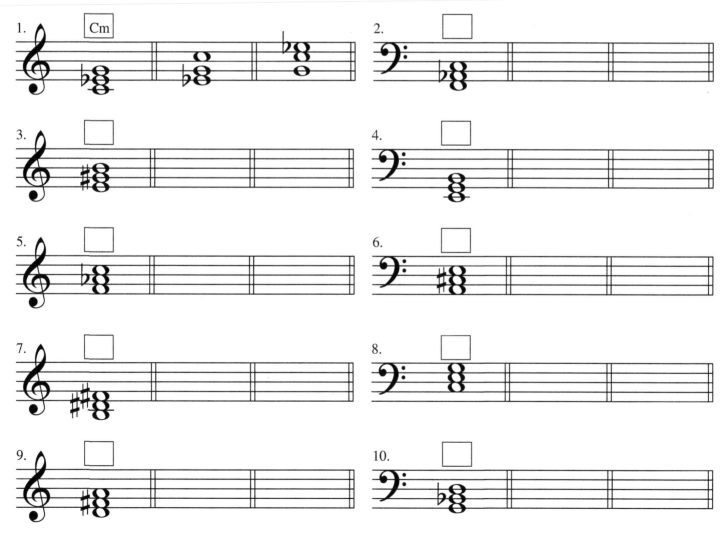

VOICE LEADING

Chord inversions add variety to the harmony in a musical composition. However, another important reason why chords are sometimes played in inversions rather than in root position relates to the advantages of improved *voice leading*. Voice leading refers to the movement of a tone in a chord to its corresponding tone in the next chord. Movement by stepwise motion (an interval of a 2nd) and stationary motion (no motion at all) in corresponding tones of consecutive chords creates a more desirable sound than does a wide leap (an interval of a 4th or greater). In order to achieve better voice leading, the employment of a mixture of root-position and inverted chords is required, rather than, say, root-position chords alone.

Examine the following example of an F major to C major chord progression. In this progression, only root-position triads are used, resulting in a descending leap of a perfect 4th from each note in the F triad to its corresponding note in the C triad. The result is generally viewed as an undesirable sound, from a voice-leading perspective.

Root-Position Triads

In the following two examples, however, the voice leading has been greatly improved. This is due to the employment of a mixture of root-position triads and inverted triads, rather than root-position triads alone, thus providing stepwise motion and stationary motion between corresponding tones of consecutive chords. This is considered to produce a much better sound.

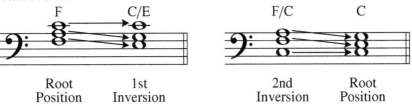

Play the following example. It features root-position chords exclusively.

Now play the same example with a mixture of root-position and inverted chords. Here, the voice leading is markedly improved. (It's also easier to play, because the left hand doesn't jump around as much as in the example above.)

Voicing: Close-Position Triads vs. Open-Position Triads

When a triad is in root position—consecutive line, line, line or consecutive space, space, space on the staff—the notes of the triad are contained within one octave and are said to be in *close position*.

By contrast, a triad may still be in root position but not be contained within one octave, due to a different chord voicing. Such a configuration of tones in a chord is called *open position*.

Here is an example of a root-position C major triad in open position, followed by a root-position C major triad in close position.

Exercises

Identify the name of each of the following root-position, open-position triads, and rewrite each of them in root position, close position. The first one is done for you.

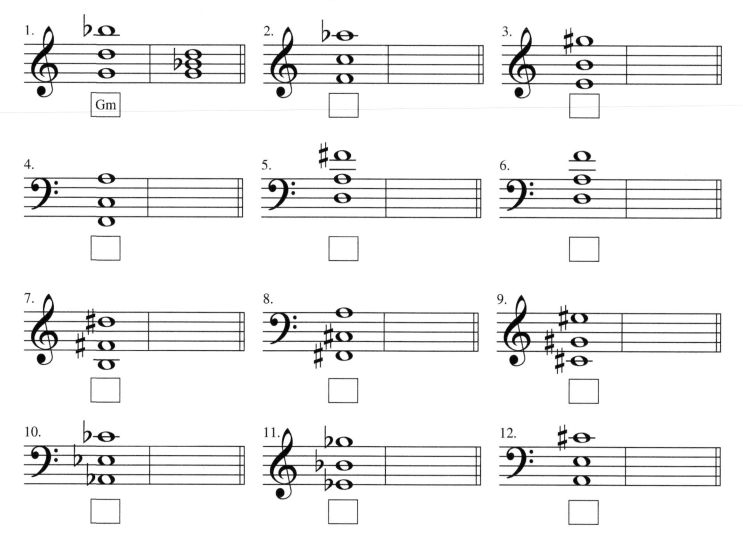

REVOICING EXERCISES

The following are several four-note chords in which one of the notes has been *doubled.* "Doubling" means that one of the pitches appears more than once. In actual practice, doubling sometimes occurs in different octaves, such as in four-part choral music—soprano, alto, tenor, and bass.

In each of the chord voicings below, there are three different pitches of a triad—a root, a 3rd, and a 5th. Through the process of trial and error, determine how these pitches can be revoiced into a root-position triad, and write the triad on consecutive lines or spaces in both the treble clef (G clef) and bass clef (F clef). Then, name the triad in the box provided. The first one is done for you.

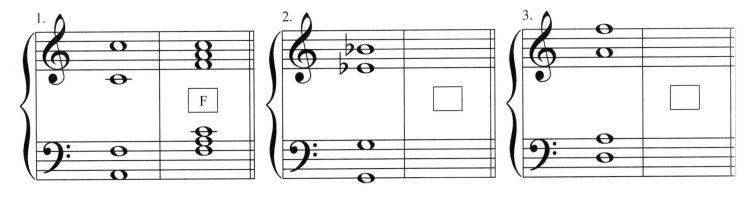

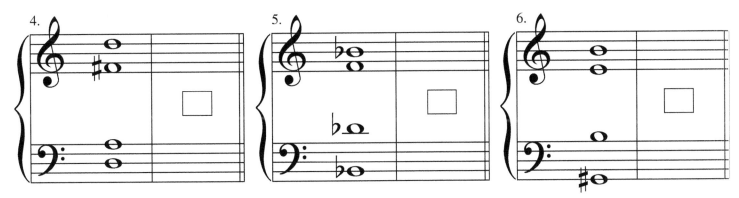

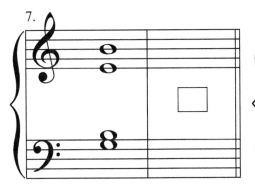
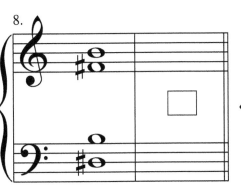
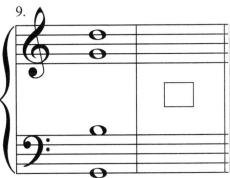

READING MUSIC FROM A LEAD SHEET

In twentieth and twenty-first century jazz and popular music, pianists have frequently been required to read music from a sketch—called a "lead sheet"—that ordinarily consists of a song's melody, alphabetical chord symbols (including Arabic numerals) over the melody, and the song's lyrics, if any.

Pianists are expected to learn how to provide a full realization from this meager information, often at sight, making spur-of-the-moment decisions regarding *voicing,* the spacing of notes in a chord (see page 10), and *voice leading* (see page 9), as that information is not provided by the chord symbols. As one can see, playing from a lead sheet is highly improvisatory in nature. One can readily locate lead sheets in bound collections of them called "fake books," so called because the word "fake" is synonymous with "improvise" in the jazz vernacular. (A tremendous proliferation of such books has occurred in recent years.)

Figured Bass

Reading music from a lead sheet has its origins in a type of chord shorthand, widely utilized during Baroque times (circa 1600–1750), called *figured bass.* In this system one sees only a bass note plus subscript numbers under it. The numbers under the bass note dictate the intervals of the notes to be played above the bass note, thus indicating the entire chord's tones as well as the chord's inversion. It was expected that the keyboard players reading this shorthand vocabulary would also improvise ornaments and embellishments appropriate to the then Baroque style.

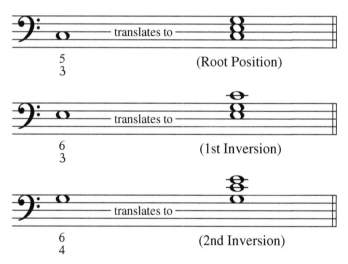

This chord shorthand system saved Baroque era composers time—what with their not having to write out all the notes—and possibly also money, as printing costs were expensive in those days. You see, composers were able to leave Baroque keyboard parts in manuscript form. In modern times, this figured bass system is used mostly for harmonic analysis in school music theory classes.

THE RELATIONSHIP OF TRIADS WITHIN A MAJOR KEY

The Harmonic System: Roman Numeral Analysis

If one were to build a triad on each note of any *major scale,* the triad built on the first, fourth, and fifth notes will always be major in quality; the triads built on the second, third, and sixth notes will always be minor in quality; and the triad built on the seventh note will always be diminished in quality. See this for yourself below.

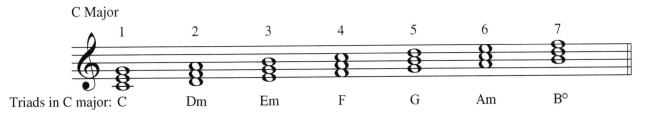

For the purpose of harmonic analysis, a triad's position within the key is indicated with Roman numerals—uppercase for major; lowercase for minor and diminished. Also note that the symbol for a diminished triad is a lowercase Roman numeral followed by a degree sign (vii°).

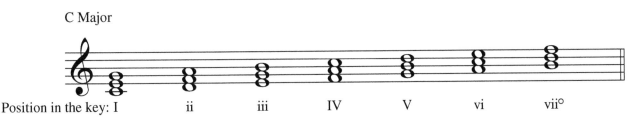

In each of the exercises below, first identify the *major* key of the key signature. (**Hint:** See page 42 of this book, in Theory Review, to remind yourself how to identify a major key from a key signature.) Then write the correct requested triad in root position (on consecutive lines or spaces). In the box above the triad that you have written, name the triad's root and quality. The first one is done for you.

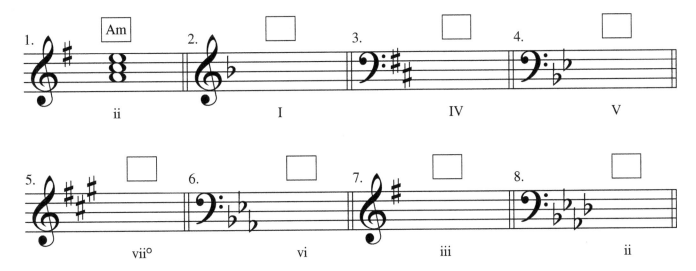

THE RELATIONSHIP OF TRIADS WITHIN A MINOR KEY

The Harmonic System: Roman Numeral Analysis

The quality of the triad built on each scale tone of a *minor scale* is different from the quality of each triad built on the equivalent tone of a major scale. (See page 13 for the quality of triads in a major key.) In a minor key, the triad built on the first, fourth, and fifth notes will always be minor in quality; the triad built on the third, sixth, and seventh notes will always be major in quality; and the triad built on the second note will always be diminished in quality. See this for yourself below.

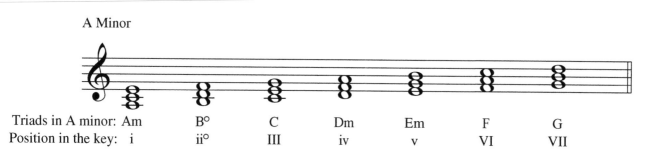

In each of the exercises below, first identify *the minor key* of the key signature. (**Hint:** See page 42 of this book, in Theory Review, to remind yourself how to identify a major key from a key signature; and then see the bottom of page 47 to remind yourself how to determine the relative minor key from any given major key.) Then write the requested minor triads in root position (on consecutive lines or spaces). In the box above the triad that you have written, name the triad's root and quality. The first one is done for you.

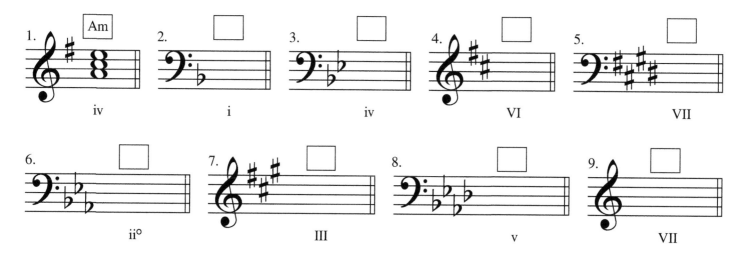

CHORD TRANSPOSITION

Being able to think in terms of Roman numerals is particularly helpful when it comes to *transposing chords* into *another key.* For example, if I'm trying to sing "Silent Night" from sheet music that happens to be published in the key of F major…

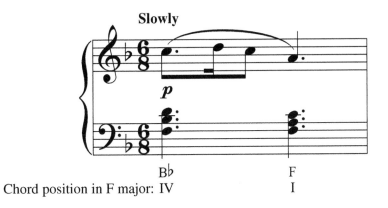

Chord position in F major: IV   I

…and find it to be much too high for my vocal range, I will transpose the melody into a lower key, say, every melody note down a perfect 5th to B♭ major. I will then think in terms of Roman numerals to help me find the comparable chords in the new key.

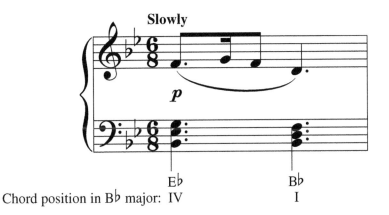

Chord position in B♭ major: IV   I

As seen above, apart from harmonic analysis, the harmonic system offers great practical value.

SLASH MARKS IN CHORD SYMBOLS

On the bottom of the next page you will encounter an interesting and useful feature of jazz and popular-music chord symbols: *slash marks.*

Slash marks serve three principal functions:

1. To indicate an *inversion:*

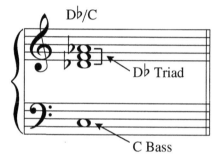

2. To indicate a *non-harmonic* tone (also known as a non-chord tone):

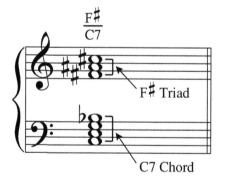

3. To indicate a polychord, a single chord comprised of two or more chords:

In this book, slash marks are employed exclusively for the purpose of indicating an inversion. However, in the book that follows this one—*How to Play Chord Symbols in Jazz and Popular Music* by Lee Evans and Martha Baker (Hal Leonard Corporation)—all three functions of slash marks are utilized.

SCALE DEGREES

The term *scale degree* refers to the various tones of a given scale. In order, they are known respectively as:

Tonic (I)

Supertonic (II)

Mediant (III)

Sub-dominant (IV)

Dominant (V)

Sub-mediant or super-dominant (VI)
  (the name of the scale tone that is halfway between the sub-dominant and upper tonic)

Sub-tonic (VII)
  (the name of the scale tone when it is a whole-step away from the upper tonic tone)

Leading tone (VII)
  (the name of the scale tone when it is one half-step away from the upper tonic tone)

SEVENTH CHORDS

As stated earlier, a triad is a three-note chord consisting of the first, third, and fifth scale degrees. By contrast, *a seventh chord is a four-note chord consisting of the first, third, fifth, and seventh scale degrees.* Just as triads have different chord qualities (major, minor, diminished, augmented), so do seventh chords also have different qualities. These will now be discussed, one by one.

Dominant 7th Chords

A *dominant 7th chord* is so-called because, as a chord built on the fifth scale degree, it is a dominating force in harmony, second in importance only to the tonic triad, the triad built on the first scale degree. That importance relates to the dominant 7th chord's strong resolution tendencies, which are discussed on page 18.

The Quality of a Dominant 7th Chord

Here are G, B, D and F, the pitches of a G7 chord—the dominant 7th chord in the key of C major—in root position and its three inversions. It is important to note that this chord in root position consists of a major triad and a minor 7th above the root. These are the interval relationships that define the *quality of a dominant 7th chord.*

NOTE: Some of the following chord symbols contain a slash mark. See page 16 for an explanation of the meaning of a slash mark in a chord symbol.

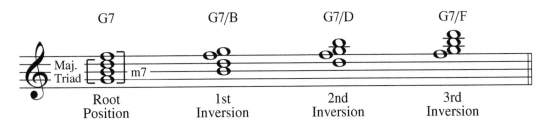

Resolution Tendencies of the Dominant 7th Chord

In tonal music (music in a particular key), the usual resolution of the dominant 7th (V7) chord is to the tonic (I) chord. This is strongly related to the presence within the dominant 7th chord of a *tritone* (three whole-steps) between two of the chord's pitches. In a G7 chord, the tritone pitches are B and F. In the key of C major, the note B—the C scale's leading tone—strongly wants to resolve to the note C, the tonic tone and root of the tonic triad. The note F—the fourth scale degree of the C major and C minor scales—wants to resolve to the third scale degree—E of the C major scale, or E♭ of the C minor scale.

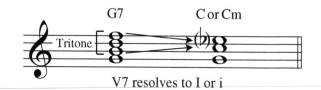

The Dominant 7th Chord in a Major Key

In a major scale, the dominant 7th chord occurs naturally when built on the fifth scale degree. That is to say, the chord comes out as a *major triad plus a minor 7th above* the root of the triad. As stated earlier, these are the interval relationships that characterize the *quality of a dominant 7th chord.*

NOTE: It is also possible for a chord to be dominant 7th in quality, even though it may not necessarily be built on the fifth scale degree of a particular scale. Examples are A7, E♭7, B♭7, etc. These chords consist of a major triad plus a minor 7th above the root of the triad, regardless of which scale degree they have been built upon.

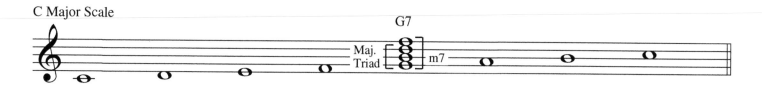

The Dominant 7th Chord in a Minor Key

The quality of a dominant 7th chord does *not* occur naturally in a minor key, as will now be shown. Here is the C natural minor scale and the 7th chord built on this scale's fifth degree. Note that it is Gm7 rather than G7:

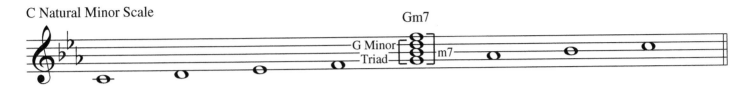

C Natural Minor Scale

Gm7

As seen above, when a 7th chord is built on the fifth note of a natural minor scale, the chord comes out as a *minor triad* plus a minor 7th above the root of the triad, instead of as a *major triad* plus a minor 7th above the root of the triad. The resolution tendencies of the traditional dominant 7th chord are thus negated because of the absence in the minor 7th chord of the interval of a tritone between any two of its pitches.

In order to create a tritone interval in a minor key, one note of the natural minor scale has to be changed. That note—the corresponding chord tone—is the scale's seventh scale degree, which has to be raised one half-step for the purpose of creating a half-step leading tone pull to the tonic tone. In other words, the natural minor scale has to be changed to a *harmonic minor scale* (which, as you know, is a natural minor scale with a raised seventh degree).

For example, here is the C harmonic minor scale with its dominant 7th chord:

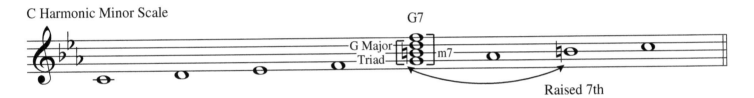

C Harmonic Minor Scale

G7

Raised 7th

The net effect of this seventh scale degree note change of the natural minor scale is that its artificially created dominant 7th chord will consist of the same pitches (G, B, D, F) as those of its parallel major key dominant 7th chord. In other words, both chords will then be dominant 7th in quality—G7.

Dominant 7th Chord Exercises in Both Major and Minor Keys

Write the following dominant 7th (V7) chords in the major or minor key given for each. First enter a key signature on the grand staff. On the keyboard above the staff, write the numbers 1, 3, 5, 7 on the respective chord tone piano keys, putting the number 1 on the root of the V7 chord. From that point, count up *four half-steps* and put the number 3 on the 3rd of the chord. From this point, count up *three half-steps* and put the number 5 on the 5th of the chord. Count up *three more half-steps* and put the number 7 on the 7th of the chord. Then write the chord on consecutive lines or spaces on the grand staff. Name the chord in the box provided and play the chord on the piano, both hands together. The first two are done for you.

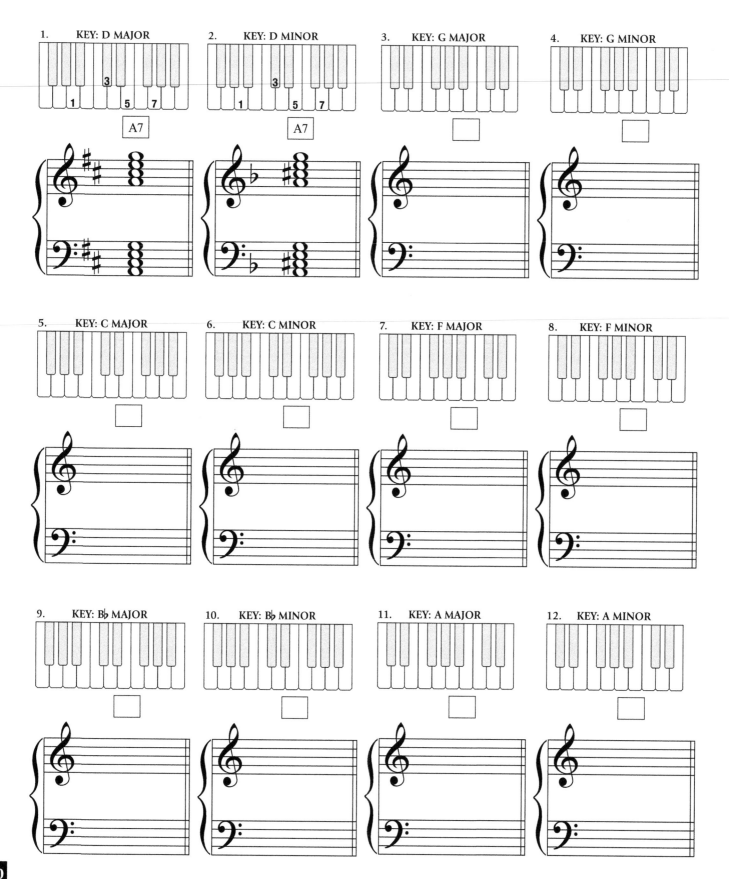

Major 7th Chords

The quality of a major 7th chord is characterized by a *major triad plus a major 7th above the root of the triad*. This chord takes its name from the root tone plus M7 (or MA7 or maj7). The tones of a major 7th chord may be viewed as having been derived from the first, third, fifth, and seventh notes of the major scale.

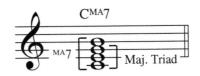

Minor 7th Chords

The quality of a minor 7th chord is characterized by a *minor triad plus a minor 7th above the root of the triad*. This chord takes its name from the root tone plus m7 (or mi7). The tones of a minor 7th chord may be viewed as having been derived from the first, third, fifth, and seventh notes of the natural minor scale.

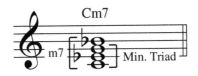

Play the following composition. It features both major 7th and minor 7th left-hand chords.

A Quiet Walk

Lee Evans

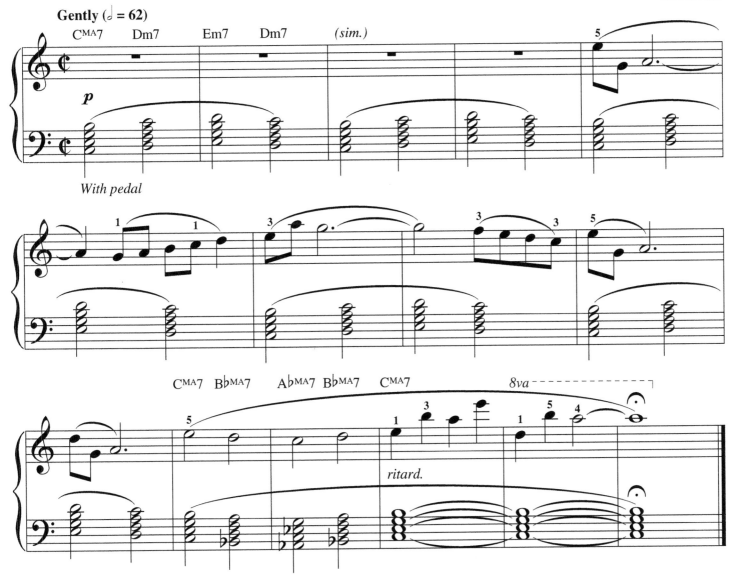

Diminished 7th Chords

The quality of a diminished 7th chord is characterized by a *diminished triad plus a diminished 7th above the root of the triad.* When analyzing a diminished 7th chord, one can see that another way of looking at it is that it consists of three minor thirds.

NOTE: In jazz and popular music, diminished chords are invariably played as four-note chords rather than as triads, whether the chord symbol says Cdim (C°) or Cdim7 (C°7).

Enharmonic spellings are frequently employed by jazz and pop musicians because they believe that by doing so, it will facilitate reading. This practice produces results that are understandably confusing to the classically trained musician. (Regrettably, breaking the rules of classical theory is a common occurrence in jazz.) Thus, while the 7th of a diminished 7th chord is a diminished 7th, it may sometimes be spelled as a major 6th. Similarly, the interval of the diminished 5th is sometimes spelled as an augmented 4th.

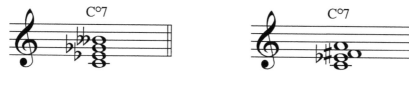

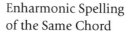

Correct Spelling   Enharmonic Spelling
of the Same Chord

Resolution Tendencies of the Diminished 7th Chord

In today's world, any chord may progress to any other chord. But in traditional functional harmony, certain chords have tended to resolve to certain other chords. The classic example of this is, of course, the dominant to tonic progression.

In functional harmony, the resolution possibilities of a diminished 7th chord are manifold, but are governed in many cases by its half-step leading-tone pull to a tonic, as in the examples below.

Because of its interval symmetry, each one of the above diminished 7th chords contains the same pitches as the other three. Also note that *any* pitch in a diminished 7th chord can resolve up a half-step to a "tonic," as shown above, making the chord extremely versatile.

Lead Sheet Performance

Practice the following four lead sheets in order to get the sound of diminished 7th chords into your ears, and the feel of the spacing of its three intervals of minor thirds in your fingers. (For broader experience, these lead sheets also feature several chords of other qualities.)

Recommended procedure:

1. Play the lead sheet chords with the left hand.
2. Play the melody in the right hand.
3. Play the melody and chords together, playing a left-hand chord wherever you see a chord symbol.

NOTE: The above procedure may be utilized for all lead sheets in this book.

I Gave My Love a Cherry

English Folk Song

St. Louis Blues

Words and Music by
W.C. Handy

Chromatic Fantasy

Lee Evans

Roses of Picardy

Words by Fred E. Weatherly
Music by Haydn Wood

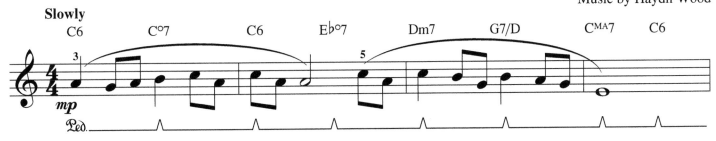

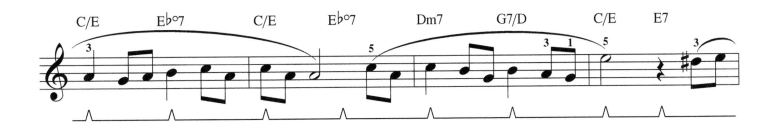

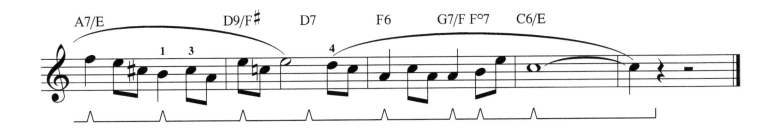

Minor 7th Chord with a Lowered 5th (Also known as a half-diminished 7th chord)

This chord consists of a *minor triad with a lowered 5th scale degree, plus a minor 7th above the root of the triad.*

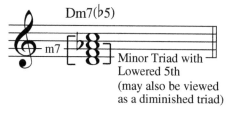

Practice the lead sheet at the bottom of this page several times in order to acquire the sound of m7(♭5) chords in your ears, in order to get the spacing of notes in chords of this quality under your fingers, and to experience playing several ii7(♭5) to V7 to I progressions.

Here is a ii7(♭5) to V7 to I progression in C major and in C minor:

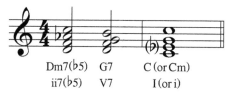

Sequences

Lee Evans

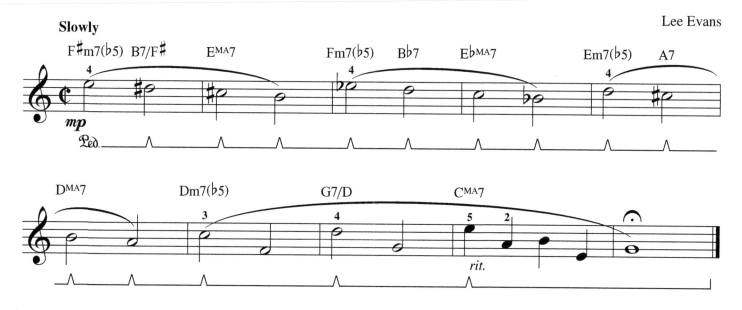

As an experiment, play the above composition employing ii7 instead of ii7(♭5) chords wherever they appear. Which version do you like better?

SUSPENSIONS

A *suspension* is a non-harmonic tone—a tone not belonging to the chord—that often resolves to the harmonic tone. In jazz harmony a suspension usually replaces the 3rd of a major or minor triad with a major 2nd or perfect 4th above the root. The normal resolution of the suspension is to the 3rd of the triad, either major or minor. Suspensions ordinarily appear in lead sheets as any of the following chord symbols:

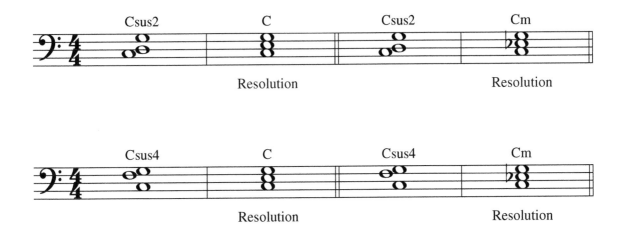

When the chord symbol for a suspension is not followed by a number (as in Csus), this generally indicates a sus4—play the 4th above the root of the chord instead of the 3rd. Occasionally, a suspension will be notated as the chord name plus an Arabic numeral, omitting the sus abbreviation (C4=Csus4).

The above suspension chords are three-note chords. However, in jazz and popular music, chords are often played as four-note chords utilizing the minor 7th above the root of the chord. Such chords appear in lead sheets as any of the following chord symbols.

Note that the ninth scale degree is identical to the second scale degree. In jazz and popular music, the 2nd is used in chord symbols only when notating sus2 chords—which don't contain the 3rd—while the 9th is used with all other chords that normally contain the 3rd.

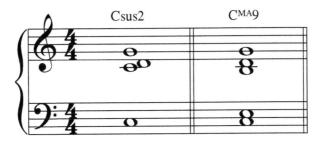

In order to get the tension-laden sound of suspensions in your ears, play the following short piece, which contains an assortment of suspension chords.

A Mixed Bag

In the exercise that follows, play the melody and chord symbols together, playing a left-hand root-position chord wherever a chord symbol appears. Write in the left-hand chords.

High Fives

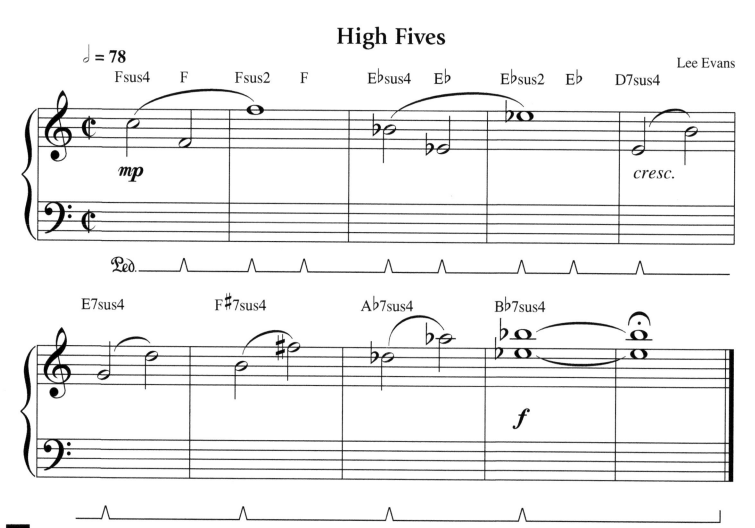

CADENCES
Resting Points in Music

Just as words are assembled into organized sentences and paragraphs for the sake of clarity of meaning, musical ideas such as *motives* (short melodic, harmonic, or rhythmic musical fragments) are assembled by composers into shapes called *phrases*. There are various ways in which phrases can be brought to a conclusion, and it is these resting points, called *cadences*, that will be discussed now.

In a manner similar to how the voice in speech inflects in a particular way in order to indicate a pause in, or the ending of, a sentence, resting points in music exist to separate musical phrases from one another, irrespective of how long or short each phrase may be. In speech as in music, the pause may be temporary (commas, semi-colons), or it may offer more of a sense of finality (period, exclamation point). Similarly, phrase endings fall into two basic categories: incomplete and complete musical thoughts. Those phrases that end on a tone that the listener perceives as not offering a sense of finality are referred to as incomplete, or imperfect, and the listener's expectation is that another phrase or additional musical material must follow. Those phrases that end on a tone that the listener perceives as offering a sense of finality—the tonic tone, or key tone (first note of the scale)—are said to be complete or perfect.

Types of Cadences

NOTE: Composers may end phrases on any pitch they please, but the examples cited below are the most typical in tonal music.

PERFECT AUTHENTIC CADENCE—A complete cadence, known as a *perfect authentic cadence,* is one in which the last two chords are V to I—dominant to tonic—and the last melody note is the key tone (first note of the scale.)

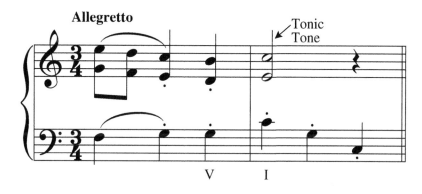

IMPERFECT AUTHENTIC CADENCE—An incomplete cadence, known as an *imperfect authentic cadence*, is one in which the last two chords are V to I—dominant to tonic—but the last melody note is the 3rd or 5th, rather than the key tone.

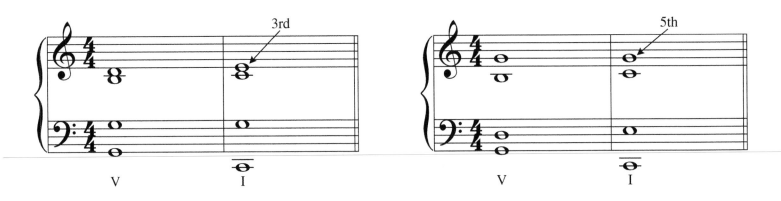

SEMI-CADENCE OR HALF-CADENCE—A temporary resting point, known as a *semi-cadence*, or *half-cadence*, is one in which the last chord of a phrase is V—the dominant chord—leading one to believe that another phrase or other additional material will follow in order to complete the musical thought.

NOTE: Another type of semi-cadence, or half-cadence, occurs when the last chord of a phrase is a IV chord, or sub-dominant chord. As an example, this substitute chord for the V chord may be heard at the end of the first phrase of "Auld Lang Syne."

PERFECT PLAGAL CADENCE—When the last two chords of a phrase are IV to I—sub-dominant to tonic—and the last melody note of the phrase is the key tone, the cadence is known as a *perfect plagal cadence*. This cadence is also known as an Amen cadence because of its traditional use at the end of hymns.

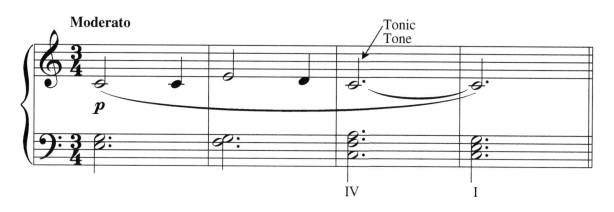

IMPERFECT PLAGAL CADENCE—When the last two chords of a phrase are IV to I—sub-dominant to tonic—and the last melody note of the phrase is the 3rd or 5th, the cadence is said to be an *imperfect plagal cadence*.

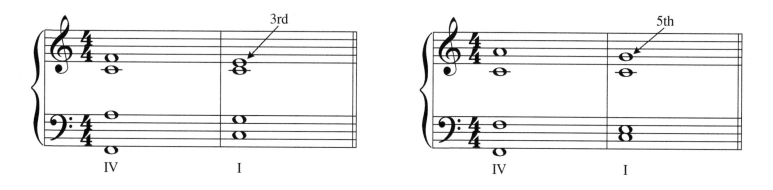

MIXED CADENCE—When an authentic cadence and plagal cadence are combined in a IV, V, I progression, it may be referred to as a *mixed cadence*.

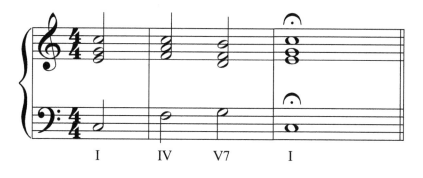

DECEPTIVE CADENCE—A *deceptive cadence* is one in which the ending of a phrase is evaded through the employment of a chord other than the tonic chord—often the VI or lowered VI chord. This causes a sense of surprise, and raises the listener's expectation that additional musical material and another cadence are required to bring the phrase to a conclusion.

Here are three cadence progressions in the key of F major. Identify each cadence as authentic, plagal, or half-cadence.

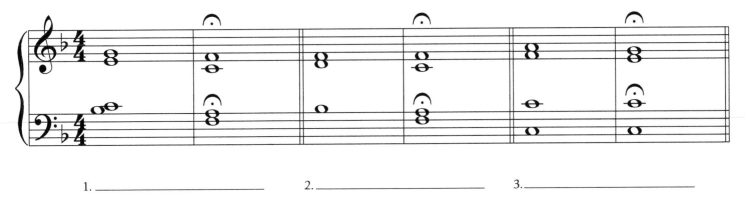

1. _____ 2. _____ 3. _____

Here are three cadence progressions in the key of D minor. Identify each cadence as authentic, plagal, or half-cadence.

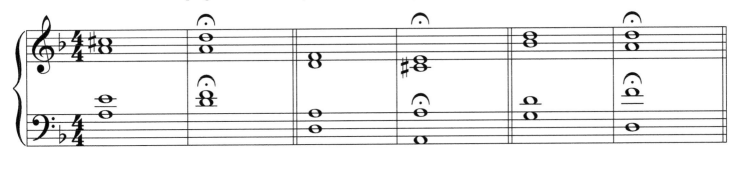

1. _____ 2. _____ 3. _____

The cadences presented here are by no means representative of all possible phrase-closing formulas throughout history. Instead, they are the ones in greatest use in the music literature of the eighteenth and nineteenth centuries. (For a more extensive discussion of cadence practice during other historical periods, refer to *The Harvard Dictionary of Music*.)

INTRODUCTION TO HARMONIZATION
The Common Tone Principle

Primary Chords

It is possible to harmonize most Western tonal music diatonic melodies (melodies using predominantly the tones of major and minor scales) by employing only three basic chords, often referred to as *primary chords*:

I CHORD (TONIC TRIAD)—the three-note chord built on the first note of the scale

IV CHORD (SUB-DOMINANT TRIAD)—the three-note chord built on the fourth note of the scale

V7 CHORD (DOMINANT 7TH CHORD)—the four-note chord built on the fifth note of the scale

Primary Chords in C Major

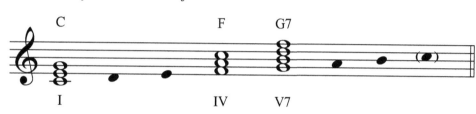

Secondary Chords

Chords built on the other scale degrees (2nd, 3rd, 6th, and 7th scale degrees) are often referred to as *secondary chords.* Their inclusion in harmonization provides more sophisticated harmonic possibilities than do primary chords alone.

Thinking Process

An effective approach to harmonization utilizing primary chords alone requires:

1. determining the key of the music to be harmonized (C major in the scale below).
2. identifying the I (C major), IV (F major), and V7 (G7) chords in that key.
3. locating a common tone between the melody tone(s) and prospective chord.

For example, let's say that you want to harmonize the tones of a C major scale:

Search for Common Tones

You notice that the note C is present in both the I (C major) and IV (F major) triads. Consequently, either chord would sound consonant (harmonious) played together with that melody note. However, due to the absence of the note C in the G7 chord, the melody note C played together with the G7 chord would sound dissonant (inharmonious) and would therefore clash. Hear this for yourself by playing the following:

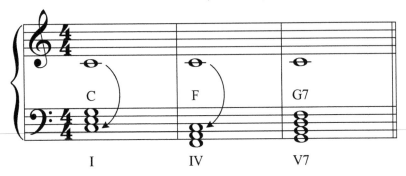

Employing the previously stated *common tone principle*, let's continue to harmonize all the tones of the C major scale with I, IV, and V7 chords only.

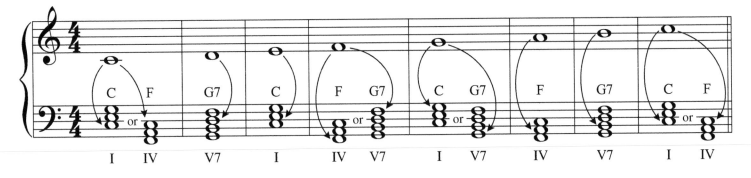

Here are my final chord choices, drawn from the above possibilities, and based upon my awareness that the melody is the C major scale and, therefore, it is in the key of C major. (For example, knowing that I'm in C major, I choose to both start and end with the I (tonic) triad.)

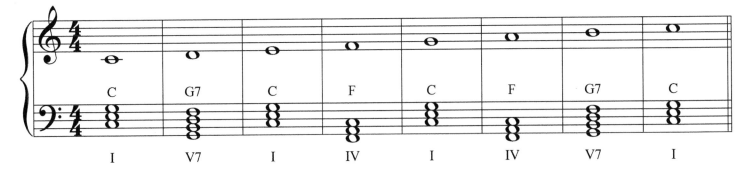

With the same chords I chose above, I'll now play them in a mixture of root position and inversions to achieve improved voice leading, a subject discussed on page 9 of this book.

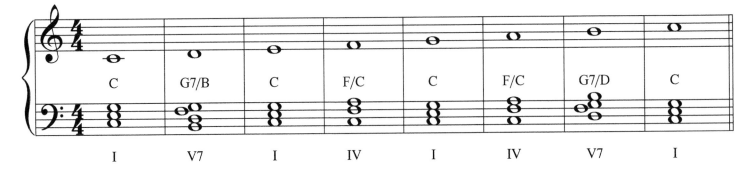

Harmonization Procedure

Here is a melody that I intend to harmonize with primary chords only, based on the common tone principle.

Procedure:

1. Determine the key of the piece (C major—rather than A minor—in the above example, based on the key signature of no sharps or flats, and on the final tone being C).

2. Locate the I, IV, and V7 chords in that key (C major (I), F major (IV), G7 (V7) in the above example).

3. Harmonize the melody based on the common tone principle, using those primary chords in root position only.

4. With the same chords, employ a mixture of root position and inversions in order to achieve the goal of improved voice leading.

(See the next page for my harmonization of the above melody.)

Harmonic Motion

Among the important decisions you will have to make in harmonization is that of how much *harmonic motion* you wish to have in your piece. By that is meant how often you want the chords to change. Do you want only one or two chords in each measure, or perhaps even fewer, or more than that? On the following page, I have put square boxes over the melody to indicate wherever I want a new chord to appear.

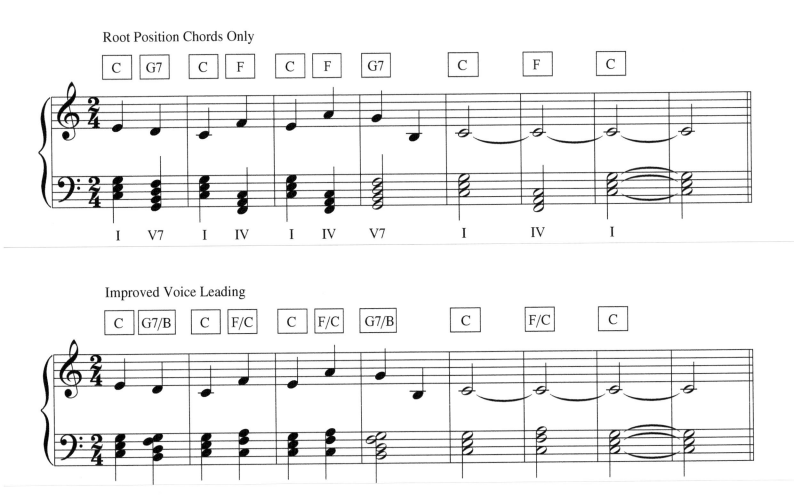

Exercises

Apply the harmonization procedure outlined on page 35 to harmonize the four melodies on the next two pages, employing only the I, IV, and V7 chords, first in root position exclusively, then in a mixture of root position and inversions in order to achieve improved voice leading. Square boxes have been placed over certain bars to indicate that this is where a chord should appear and should be sustained until the next square box appears.

NOTE: Two of the following harmonization examples are in a major key and two are in a minor key.
  On page 14, the quality of triads in a minor key was discussed. Keep in mind that in a minor key:

- the i chord is minor.
- the iv chord is minor.
- but the V7 chord will be dominant 7th in quality.
  (See page 19 for a discussion of dominant 7th chords in a minor key.)

Harmonization Exercises

Harmonize the melodies on this page with primary chords only (I, IV, V7) in root position. Then, using the same chords, improve the voice leading through the use of a mixture of root position chords and chords in inversions. (Reminder: First determine the key of each piece; then identify the three primary chords in that key; then select the appropriate chord(s) in each bar based on the common tone principle described earlier in this Introduction to Harmonization section of the book.)

Example 1a (Chords in Root Position)

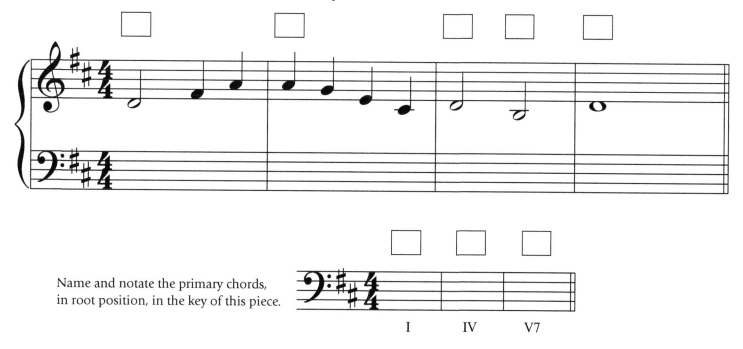

Name and notate the primary chords, in root position, in the key of this piece.

I   IV   V7

Example 1b

With the same chord choices used above, now improve the voice leading.

Example 2a (Chords in Root Position)

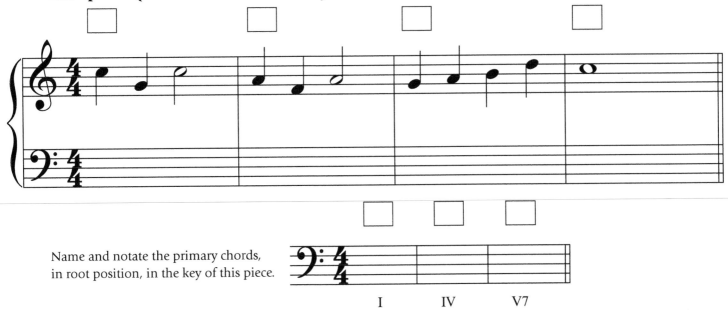

Name and notate the primary chords, in root position, in the key of this piece.

I   IV   V7

Example 2b

With the same chord choices used above, now improve the voice leading.

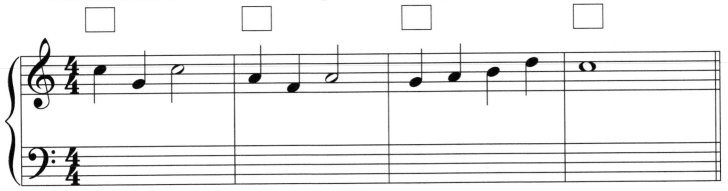

Example 3a (Chords in Root Position)

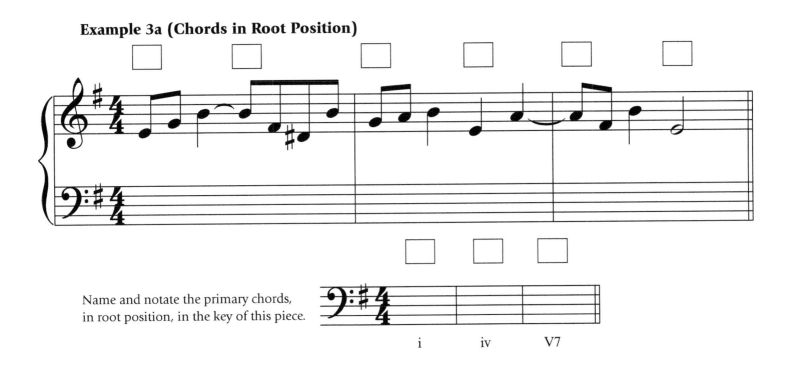

Name and notate the primary chords, in root position, in the key of this piece.

i   iv   V7

Example 3b

With the same chord choices used in Example 3a, now improve the voice leading.

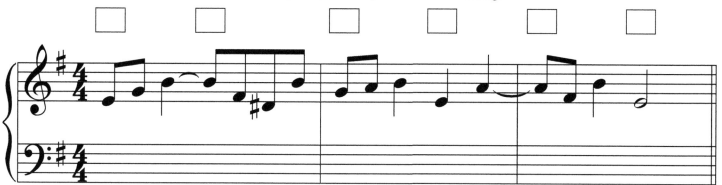

Example 4a (Chords in Root Position)

Name and notate the primary chords,
in root position, in the key of this piece.

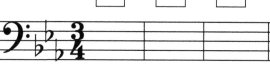

        i   iv   V7

Example 4b

With the same chord choices used above, now improve the voice leading.

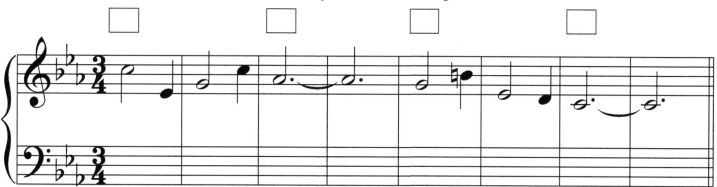

You are now ready to proceed to the follow-up book, ***How to Play Chord Symbols in Jazz and Popular Music*** by Lee Evans and Martha Baker (HAL LEONARD CORPORATION). That book develops facility in reading alphabetical chord symbols at the keyboard.

Part I of that volume teaches and provides practical performance opportunities in basic chords up to and including various types of 7th chords and altered chords—chords in which one or more notes have been raised or lowered one half-step.

Part II of that volume teaches and provides performance opportunities in the most frequently used extended chords—9ths, 11ths, and 13th chords—as well as additional chords.

HL00009080

THEORY REVIEW

Major and Minor Scales—Diatonic Scales

Major scales and *minor scales* are successions of tones that form the basis of tonal music (music in a particular key). Both types of scales are *diatonic scales*. This means that:

1. These scales each have five whole-steps and two half-steps. The major scales and minor scales have different formulas for the arrangement of those intervals. The major scale interval formula appears at the bottom of this page; the minor scale interval formula is shown on page 46.

2. In constructing major scales, the next letter of the musical alphabet is always used, without omitting or repeating an alphabet letter. This principle forces the choice of the correct enharmonic name for each note of the scale as the scales are being built.

3. The next available line or space on the musical staff is used, without omitting or repeating a line or space.

Visualizing a Piano Keyboard

It is essential to be able to visualize the layout of a piano keyboard, especially in constructing scales. Here is a diagram of a piano keyboard:

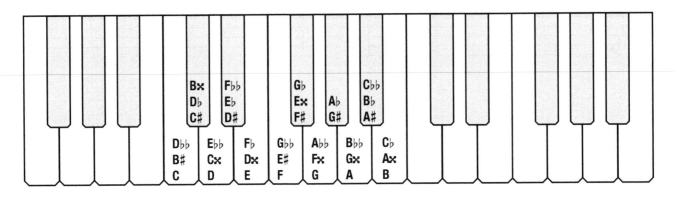

Every key on the keyboard has three enharmonic names except for G♯/A♭, which has only two.

Interval Formula of Major Scales

On the next page appear major scales in treble clef, one octave ascending. Major scales use the exact same notes descending as ascending. Notice that each scale contains one sharp or flat more than the preceding one. The following interval formula of whole-steps and half-steps is employed in constructing major scales:

Tonic Tone	1	1	½	1	1	1	½

Notice that half-steps occur only between scale degrees 3–4 and 7–8 in major scales.

Major Scales

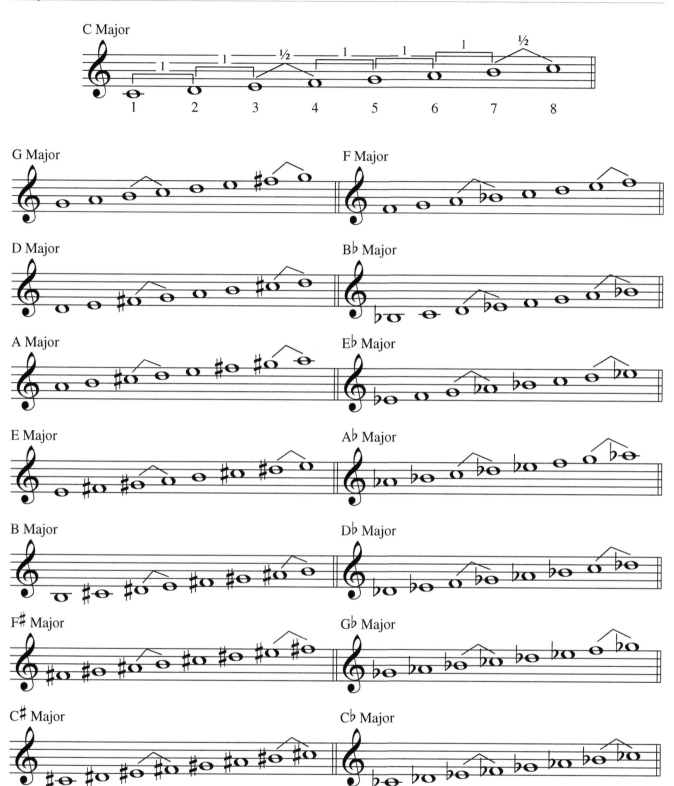

Major Scale Key Signatures

Major Keys

The Order of Sharps

What is the rationale for F♯ always being the first sharp in a key signature having sharps; why is C♯ always the second sharp; G♯ always the third sharp, etc.? The answer follows a very easy formula.

The major scale that contains only one sharp (G major) uses F♯. The major scale that contains two sharps (D major) uses the same F♯, plus C♯. The major scale that contains three sharps (A major) uses the same F♯ and C♯, plus G♯, etc. Note that in this scheme the next sharp in a key signature is always determined by counting *five musical alphabet letters forward*:

> F♯ (f, g, a, b, **c**)
>
> C♯ (c, d, e, f, **g**)
>
> G♯ (g, a, b, c, **d**)
>
> D♯ (d, e, f, g, **a**)
>
> A♯ (a, b, c, d, **e**)
>
> E♯ (e, f, g, a, **b**)
>
> B♯ (b, c, d, e, **f**)

RULE: When one sees music having a key signature containing sharps, the key of the piece is a diatonic (next alphabet letter) half-step higher than the name of the last sharp.

For example, if the key signature consists of three sharps, F♯, C♯, and G♯, the key is A major—a diatonic half-step higher than the name of the last sharp (G♯) in the key signature.

The Order of Flats

The rationale for the order of flats in a key signature having flats is the following:

The major scale that contains only one flat (F major) uses B♭. The major scale that contains two flats (B♭ major) uses the same B♭, plus E♭. The major scale that contains three flats (E♭ major) uses the same B♭ and E♭, plus A♭, and so on. Note that in this scheme the next flat in a key signature is always determined by counting *five musical alphabet letters backward*:

> B♭ (b, a, g, f, **e**)
>
> E♭ (e, d, c, b, **a**)
>
> A♭ (a, g, f, e, **d**)
>
> D♭ (d, c, b, a, **g**)
>
> G♭ (g, f, e, d, **c**)
>
> C♭ (c, b, a, g, **f**)
>
> F♭ (f, e, d, c, **b**)

RULE: When one sees music having a key signature containing only one flat, B♭, one has to memorize that that is the key signaure for F major. Thereafter, however, the name of the key of the music is the name of the next-to-last flat in the key signature.

For example, if the key signature consists of two flats—B♭, and E♭—the key is B♭ major, the name of the next-to-last flat. If the key signature consists of three flats—B♭, E♭, and A♭—the key is E♭ major, the name of the next-to-last flat.

INTERVALS

An *interval* is *a measurement of the distance between any two pitches,* either played consecutively (called a melodic interval) or simultaneously (called a harmonic interval). Interval size is determined by counting staff lines and spaces from one note to another.

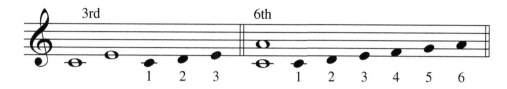

However, counting staff steps, as shown above, is not an exact enough interval measurement. That can be illustrated as follows:

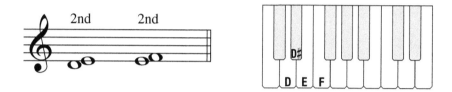

Both of the above intervals are 2nds, but D–E is a larger 2nd because it encompasses two half-steps. By contrast, E–F is a smaller 2nd because it encompasses only one half-step.

A more precise measurement of intervals may be accomplished through designation of two different elements: *quality* (major, minor, perfect, diminished, augmented) and *the number of staff lines and spaces.*

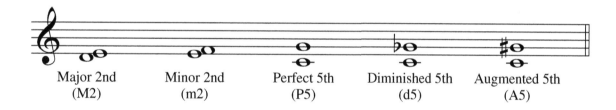

Interval Formula

An extremely effective method for determining an exact interval name (quality plus number) involves thinking of a major scale—say C major—and combining each tone of that scale with the tonic tone (first note) of the same scale.

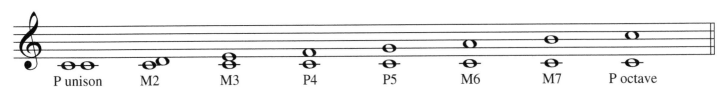

As shown above, combining the tonic tone of any major scale with itself (an interval called a unison), with the fourth and fifth notes of the same scale, and with its octave note result in what are referred to as *perfect* intervals: Perfect unison, Perfect 4th, Perfect 5th, Perfect octave.*

Also as shown above, combining the tonic tone of any major scale with the 2nd, 3rd, 6th, and 7th notes of the same scale result in what are referred to as *major* intervals: Major 2nd, Major 3rd, Major 6th, Major 7th.

Basic Interval Rules

1. A *perfect interval made smaller* by one half-step produces an interval called *diminished*.

2. A *perfect interval made larger* by one half-step produces an interval called *augmented*.

3. A *major interval made smaller* by one half-step produces an interval called *minor*.

4. A *minor interval made larger* by one half-step produces an interval called *major*.

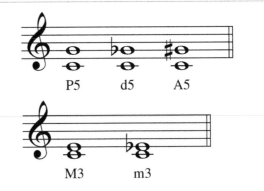

Basic Rules for Intervals of Less Frequent Occurrence

5. A *major interval made larger* by one half-step is called *augmented*.

6. A *minor interval made smaller* by one half-step is called *diminished*.

---

*In the Middle Ages, the intervals of the unison, 4th, 5th, and octave were the only ones thought to be musical (harmonious), while all other intervals were thought to be unmusical (inharmonious). Even though this perception has changed dramatically over the years, the term "perfect" has continued to be employed.

Applying the Rules Regarding Intervals

If asked to state the *quality and number* of a given interval, say D up to F…

…think of a major scale starting on the lower note of the interval—the D major scale in the example above.

D Major

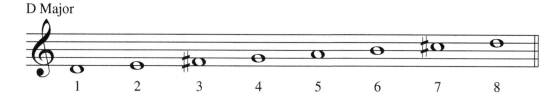

1   2   3   4   5   6   7   8

Ask yourself if the top note of the interval is a scale tone in that scale. Then apply the Interval Formula from the top of page 44. For example, with respect to the above interval, I notice that the third note of the D major scale is F♯, not F. If the top note of the interval in question had been F♯, then the interval would be called a major 3rd, according to the Interval Formula. But D up to F is smaller than a major 3rd. According to Basic Interval Rule #3 in the middle of page 44, a major interval made smaller by one half-step produces a minor interval. Therefore, the above interval is called a *minor 3rd.*

Applying the same thinking process to another interval, say F up to B…

…think of the F major scale (the major scale of the interval's lower note).

F Major

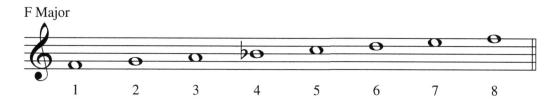

1   2   3   4   5   6   7   8

Ask yourself if B—the top note of the interval in question—is a scale tone in the F major scale. Then apply the Interval Formula at the top of page 44. For example, I notice that the fourth note of the F major scale is B♭, not B. If the top note of the interval in question had been B♭, then the interval would be called a perfect 4th, according to the Interval Formula. But F up to B is a half-step larger than a perfect 4th. According to Basic Interval Rule #2 in the middle of page 44, a perfect interval made larger by one half-step produces an augmented interval. Therefore, the above interval is an *augmented 4th.*

Knowing the language of intervals is essential in identifying chords because, as with intervals, chords are also identified by *quality* (C *major,* for example). The quality of a chord is the function of the interval relationships in that chord. For example, a major triad (say C major) consists of a root (C), a major 3rd (E), and a perfect 5th (G).

MINOR SCALES

As stated earlier, *minor scales*—like major scales—are *diatonic scales* in that they have five whole-steps and two half-steps; they use the next alphabet letter, without omitting or repeating an alphabet letter; and the notes are written in succession on the next available staff line or space, without omitting or repeating a staff line or space.

Interval Formula of Minor Scales

The following formula of whole-steps and half-steps is employed in constructing minor scales:

Tonic Tone   1   ½   1   1   ½   1   1

Notice that the half-steps occur only between scale steps 2–3 and 5–6 in the minor scale.

Here is the A natural minor scale. It uses the same pitches descending as ascending.

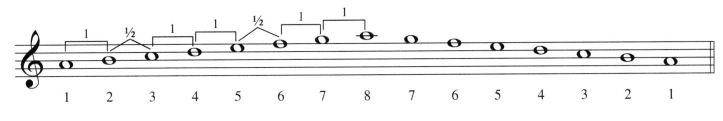

Natural Minor Scale

In a *major scale,* the interval of a half-step occurs between scale degrees 7 and 8. When the seventh scale degree is only a half-step away from the tonic tone, the seventh degree is then called a *leading tone* because there is a strong sense of urgency for it to lead to, or move to, the tonic tone.

In a *minor scale,* however, the interval of a whole-step, rather than one half-step, occurs between scale degrees 7 and 8. Thus there is a much less compelling sense of movement from the seventh scale degree to the tonic tone. Composers liked the minor scale a lot, but were dismayed by that one aspect of it: the whole-step distance between scale steps 7 and 8. As a result, composers created two altered minor scales that would correct for that perceived "flaw." The unaltered version of the minor scale thus came to be known as the *natural minor scale,* the term "natural" in this context meaning "pure," or unaltered. The two altered minor scales came to be known, respectively, as *harmonic minor* and *melodic minor.*

Harmonic Minor Scale

The *harmonic minor scale* raises the seventh note of the natural minor scale one half-step and uses the same pitches descending as ascending.

NOTE: The key signature employed for the harmonic minor scale is that of the natural minor scale. The raised seventh pitch in this altered scale uses an accidental within the body of any music based on this scale.)

A Harmonic Minor Scale

Melodic Minor Scale

The *melodic minor scale* is an unusual scale in that it uses different pitches descending than it does ascending. Ascending, the sixth and seventh notes of the natural minor scale are each raised one half-step. Descending, however, those raised pitches are lowered one half-step each, thus restoring them back to the pitches of the original natural minor scale.

NOTE: The key signature employed for the melodic minor scale is that of the natural minor scale. The raised pitches in this altered scale use accidentals within the body of any music based on this scale.

Minor Scale Key Signatures

Minor Keys

Each key signature may represent not one, but two possible keys: a major key or its relative minor key. In order to determine the relative minor key from a major key, find the sixth scale degree of the major scale. The name of that note is the name of the relative minor key.

For example, the sixth note of the B♭ major scale is G. Therefore, G minor is the relative minor of B♭ major. Both of these keys utilize the identical key signature of two flats: B♭ and E♭.

Conversely, if you try to determine the relative major key from a minor key, find the third note of the minor scale. The name of that note is the name of the relative major key.

For example, the third note of the C minor scale is E♭. Therefore, E♭ major is the relative major of C minor. Both of these keys utilize the identical key signature of three flats: B♭, E♭, and A♭.

When introducing a new piece of music to students, I always ask them to first look at the key signature, and then tell me the two possible keys the piece may be in, and then look at the last chord of the piece. In tonal music (music that sounds as though it's in a particular key), the historical custom and practice has been that the music invariably ends on the tonic chord (the chord built on the first degree of the scale). As an example, if a piece with no sharps or flats ends on a C major chord, one should assume that the piece is in C major. However, if the last chord is instead A minor, one should assume that the piece is in A minor, the relative minor of C major.

Natural Minor Scales

MAJOR VS. MINOR

The principal difference between major and minor scales in terms of sound is the difference heard in the interval of the *major 3rd from the first to the third note of the major scale*, compared to the interval of the *minor 3rd from the first to the third note of the minor scale*. This vast difference is especially pronounced in the realm of chords.

ANSWER KEY

Major and Minor Triads—Page 5

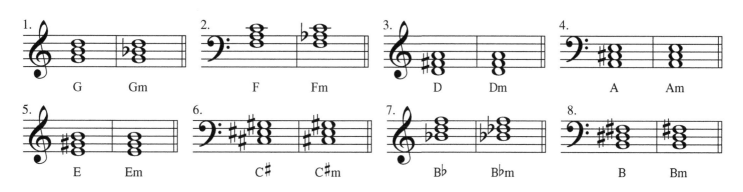

1. G   Gm
2. F   Fm
3. D   Dm
4. A   Am
5. E   Em
6. C♯   C♯m
7. B♭   B♭m
8. B   Bm

Diminished and Augmented Triads—Page 5

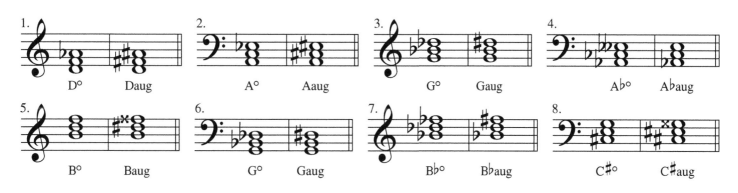

1. D°   Daug
2. A°   Aaug
3. G°   Gaug
4. A♭°   A♭aug
5. B°   Baug
6. G°   Gaug
7. B♭°   B♭aug
8. C♯°   C♯aug

Triad Inversion Exercises—Page 8

Close Position vs. Open Position Triads—Page 10

Revoicing Exercises—Page 11

Harmonic System/Triads in a Major Key—Page 13

Harmonic System/Triads in a Minor Key—Page 14

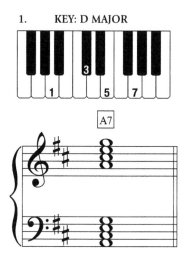
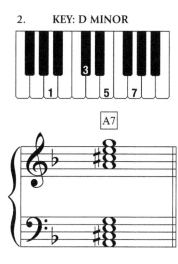
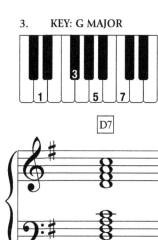
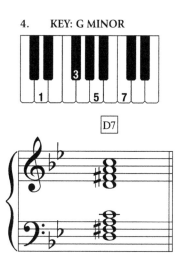
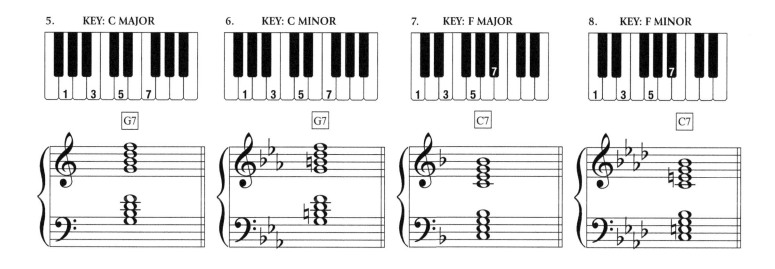
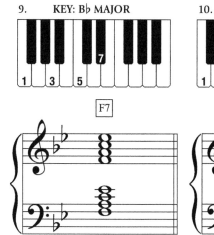

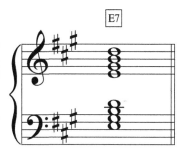

"High Fives"/Suspensions—Page 28

Lee Evans

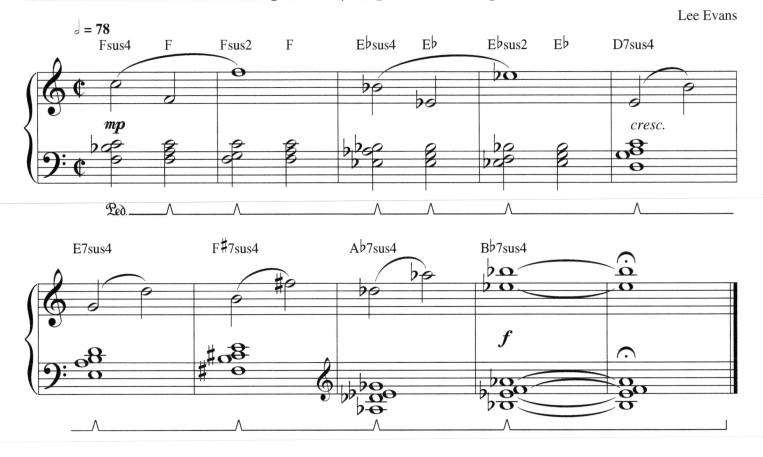

Cadences—Page 32

F Major

1. Perfect Authentic Cadence   2. Perfect Plagal Cadence   3. Half- (Semi-) Cadence

D Minor

1. Perfect Authentic Cadence   2. Half- (Semi-) Cadence   3. Perfect Plagal Cadence

Example 1a

Example 1b (this is only one of several possible solutions.)

Example 2a

Example 2b (this is only one of several possible solutions.)

Example 3a

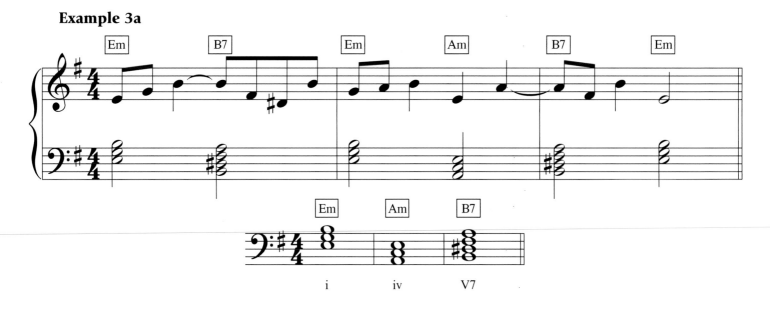

Harmonization Exercises—Page 39

Example 3b (this is only one of several possible solutions.)

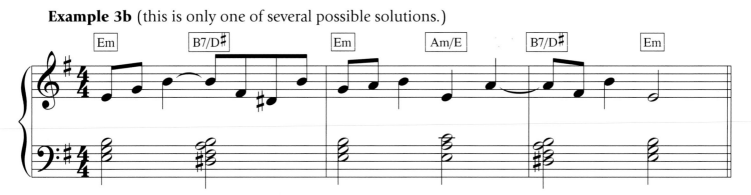

Example 4a

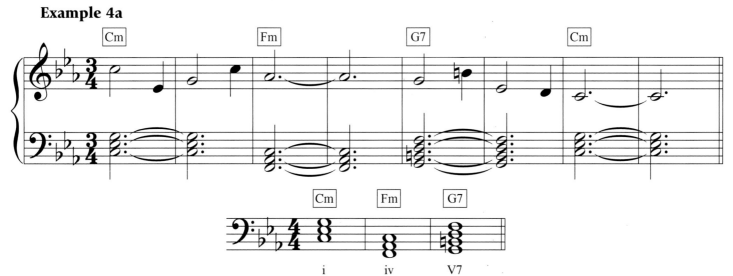

Example 4b (this is only one of several possible solutions.)